Personal Development and Work Experience Guide

Personal, Learning and Thinking Skills for the 21st Century

Edited by
John Mainstone and Ken Reynolds

Personal Development and Work Experience Guide
This edition published in 2007 by Cambridge Occupational Analysts Ltd
Sparham, Norwich, NR9 5PR

Editorial and Publishing Team

By John Mainstone and Ken Reynolds
Design and typesetting Simon Foster and Paul Rankin

© Cambridge Occupational Analysts 2007

British Library Cataloguing in Publication Data
A catalogue record for this book is available from the British Library.

ISBN 978-0-9550541-6-7

Typeset by Cambridge Occupational Analysts Ltd, Sparham, Norwich NR9 5PR
Printed and bound in Great Britain by Clays Ltd, Bungay, Suffolk NR35 1ED

Disclaimer

While every effort has been made by the publishers to ensure that all information in this book is up-to-date and accurate, and that all organisations listed are *bona fide* providers of opportunities for young people to develop their personal, learning and thinking skills, inclusion of these should not necessarily be assumed to be a recommendation that they will be suitible in all cases.

The authors do not accept any liability for errors, omissions or apparently misleading statements, nor for any loss, illness, injury or inconvenience resulting from the use of the information supplied. Readers must research all options with extreme thoroughness and reach their own judgment regarding the implications involoved, risks, costs and suitibility.

Contents

Introduction

This book is about how you can develop your abilities in ways that will help you succeed in your future career. It is aimed primarily at young people aged around 16 to 18. We envisage that most readers will be working towards GCSEs, AS/A levels, Highers or equivalent and will be applied for in Year 11, 12 or 13, Scottish Year 4 or 5 at school or college. You may be starting to research possible courses in higher education, perhaps contemplating a Gap Year before going to university, and wondering what on earth you'll be able to write in your UCAS application that will have admissions tutors queuing up to recruit such an admirable student!

Our goal is to present you with a series of suggestions and exercises that will give you an idea of the many opportunities available and an understanding of how best to match these opportunities to your own needs.

Should you wish to improve your grades by re-taking examinations or by seeking extra tuition for your current studies, we list colleges offering this type of provision. We also give details of Taster courses, provided by many universities and colleges to allow you to experience something of the academic and social life of an undergraduate student before you make a formal application - normally in years 12 or 13 Sixth Form.

Key Skills

Whatever you decide to do, try to look beyond the admittedly important elements of fun and excitement to think about whether your chosen activities will help develop the key skills needed for success in education, training, work and life in general.

Some commonly recognised key skills are:

Application of number

Communication - verbal and written

Learning

Applying information and communication technology

Problem solving and innovation

Working with others - leadership and teamwork

These are relevant for everyone, from the youngest pupils in school to the most senior executives in large organisations. With the help of this book, not to mention time spent analysing your needs and exploring appropriate options, you should be able to improve the quality of your learning and performance by applying these skills in different contexts.

You should already have some knowledge of key skills, perhaps linked with a work experience programme in your school or college, together with curriculum enrichment activities. Key skills are also developed in the workplace and as part of university degree programmes. Not least, the achievement of key skills is recognised in the UCAS tariff for admission to higher education courses.

List any five important skills you don't feel that you currently possess, or would like to reinforce, then think about how you could become involved in activities which would help you develop those skills.

If you can provide examples from your own experience to illustrate some of the qualities encapsulated in the statements, you will find that you have much of the material needed to complete the Personal Statement section of your university application. For more information on this, see our companion volume '40 Successful Personal Statements for University Application' by Guy and Gavin Nobes.

By tackling some of the projects outlined in this book, you could to learn to lead with respect, to plan with safety and to participate with enthusiasm.

Widen your interests and develop your Abilities!

Once you feel motivated to develop your personal, learning and thinking skills, spend some time exploring the websites of the organisations listed on the following pages. The sheer number of agencies can be bewildering, so we have grouped them under headings to help you become aware of the range of opportunities available and decide what sort of activity best meets your needs. Please note, however, that many organisations offer such a variety of opportunities that they could easily be placed under several headings.

You can spend your time in the UK or overseas; you may be paid or you may have to pay a considerable sum in order to participate; you may choose a course of study or you may go on an expedition. Or maybe you've simply been stuck in the classroom for too long! Time to get out in the fresh air and discover the delights of the great outdoors. It could be environmental work, sports coaching, working in a medical mission, joining an expedition, investigating a rain forest, gaining valuable business skills. The choice and opportunity are yours.

The Geographical Index will show you how many different countries offer opportunities. The Taster Course Index could prove an invaluable source of ideas for your choice of course and university, when you could explore the daily life of an undergraduate at university.

Community Projects

The aim of these projects is usually to offer humanitarian aid to communities living in poverty, to provide healthcare for the chronically sick, to rebuild homes destroyed by floods and so on. Some schemes ask for volunteers with skills in, say, construction or healthcare. In some cases you may have to raise funding for an overseas venture - but this itself can be an invaluable experience amd demonstration of your determination to participate

lst plus   17+

With a lst Plus cultural exchange programme you can work, study, travel or teach in locations throughout the world. Work in the USA, teach in Thailand or China, travel around Australia and New Zealand, or study a language anywhere in the world.

www.istplus.com

Adventure Jobs 16+

If you are looking for a job in adventure activity, travel, watersports or skiing, you may find something suitable here. The site lists vacancies for activity instructors, group leaders, centre managers, resort staff, chefs, nannies, receptionists, drivers and support staff, among many others.

www.adventurejobs.co.uk

Africa and Asia Venture 18-24

AV, as it is generally known, recruits 18-24 year olds, who want to combine four to five months of travel, safaris, adventure, friendship and fun in a year out with teaching in rural primary or secondary schools, coaching sports in rural primary or secondary schools, working with local communities or conservation work in the bush and on the Indian Ocean. You would normally start with a four-day in-country training course, then spend three to four months at your project, followed by one month of travel and safari. The latter could include seeing wildlife in African National Parks, visiting temples and palaces in India and Nepal, or adventure in Mexico. In Thailand, you would teach among the hill tribes for two months, followed by one month's project work, three weeks of travel/adventure opportunities and a five-day open water diving course.

www.aventure.co.uk

African Conservation Experience 17+

African Conservation Experience claims to be the most experienced organisation for conservation placements in Southern Africa. It can offer you the chance to work on game and nature reserves alongside conservationists, zoologists, wildlife vets and reserve managers. The organisation welcomes volunteers from all backgrounds, with no previous experience necessary, from the age of 17 upwards. Volunteer Placements are from one to three months, and you can combine two or more projects in one trip. You could join a placement as part of a Gap Year, in a summer break from school or university, or as part of a career break or sabbatical.

www.conservationafrica.net

Au Pair in America   18+

Working as an au pair in America can be a good way to discover the USA, as you can experience everyday life with a carefully selected American family and earn weekly pocket money by providing childcare as a nanny or babysitter. Whether you're looking for a year out or just want to work legally abroad, the exchange programmes on the Au Pair in America website give you free time to explore, study, travel and make new friends, together with professional support throughout your stay.

www.aupairinamerica.com

Blue Ventures

A not-for-profit organisation dedicated to facilitating projects and expeditions that enhance global marine conservation and research, Blue Ventures coordinates expeditions consisting of scientists and volunteers, working hand-in-hand with local biologists, governmental departments and communities, to carry out research, environmental awareness and conservation programmes at threatened marine habitats around the world.

www.blueventures.org

British Trust for Conservation Volunteers   All ages

BTCV has a successful history of environmental conservation volunteering throughout the UK and around the world. BTCV holidays take place all year round in some of the world's finest landscapes. Living, laughing and cooking together, you'll be busy all over, all the time. BTCV holidays don't just improve the environment - they're good for your health and could change your life.

www.btcv.org

BUNAC   18+

BUNAC offers a range of working holidays, including a summer camp counselling programme in the USA and Canada, flexible work and travel programmes to Canada, the USA, Australia, New Zealand and South Africa and volunteering/teaching placements. These are open to 18 year-olds and over in the UK, the USA and Ireland. Programmes last from five weeks to two years.

www.bunac.org

Camp America   18+

Each year over 7,500 young people take the opportunity to join Camp America and spend the summer in the USA, living and working either with children or 'behind the scenes' as support staff on an American Summer Camp. Following the end of your placement, you'll have up to two months to travel (in total your visa allows for up to four months placement followed by one month of travel but most placements end well within four months).

www.campamerica.co.uk

Changing Worlds   17+

With a wide variety of paid and voluntary placements worldwide, Changing Worlds offers destinations ranging from Australia, China and Ghana to Honduras, India, Kenya, Latvia, Madagascar, New Zealand and Thailand.

www.changingworlds.co.uk

Cathedral Camps 16-25

Experience the hidden history of some of Britain's oldest and most beautiful buildings. Cathedrals, abbeys, minsters, chapels and parish churches make up a huge part of Britain's architectural heritage and every year teams of young people from all over the world move in to help refresh and conserve these buildings. Cathedral Camps have been running week-long residential breaks at cathedrals and churches throughout the UK for over 20 years - there are on average 20 camps at different venues, running each year throughout July and August. Cathedral Camps is now run by the UK volunteering agency CSV (Community Service Volunteers), mentioned elsewhere in this publication.

www.cathedralcamps.org.uk

Community Service Volunteers 16+

The UK's largest volunteering and training organisation, CSV provides hundreds of full-time volunteering opportunities across the UK that will equip you with life skills and enhance your CV or UCAS application. You will spend 4-12 months living away from home, supporting people in need and enabling them to develop or manage their own lives. As a CSV volunteer you will take on an important role that is valued by the community. You can use your skills and develop new ones, test yourself out in new situations, challenge your way of thinking, and make a genuine and positive impact on people's lives. CSV's placements are community-based, supporting a wide variety of people. You may be helping people with physical disabilities, learning difficulties, elderly people or supporting children or young people.

www.csv.org.uk

Concordia 16-30

In addition to UK farm placements, Concordia offers an extensive international volunteer programme. Short-term projects bring together individuals from around the world to participate in two- to four-week projects in Western, Eastern and Central Europe, North America, North Africa, Japan and South Korea or Africa, Asia and Latin America. Medium-term projects usually last between one and six months, although they occasionally last for a whole year.

www.concordia-iye.org.uk

Coral Cay Conservation 16+

Coral Cay Conservation (CCC) is a not-for-profit organisation at the cutting edge of ecotourism. It sends teams of volunteers to survey some of the world's most endangered coral reefs and tropical forests. Its mission is to protect these crucial environments by working closely with the local communities who depend on them for food and livelihood. CCC currently has coral reef expeditions in Tobago and the Philippines and forest expeditions in the Philippines and Papua New Guinea. The organisation is largely financed by volunteers, who pay to participate in an expedition for anything from one week upwards. Volunteers require no scientific background and are trained on-site in marine or terrestrial ecology and survey techniques.

www.coralcay.org

European Voluntary Service 18-25

The European Voluntary Service (EVS) is an Action of the Youth programme, implemented by the European Commission and YOUTH National Agencies. It allows young people to do a voluntary service in a local host organisation in a foreign country. Each year, about 4000 volunteers participate in EVS. The annual funding is more than 300 million euro. The volunteer gains a variety of personal, professional and intercultural skills, and brings some added value and intercultural flavour to the gost organisation and local comminity.

www.sosforevs.org

Experiment in International Living   16+

Your community service as an EIL Volunteer for International Partnership (VIP) could be working with a rural development project, volunteering in a health clinic, working with children or teaching English. VIP offers individuals or groups the opportunity to volunteer abroad in 14 countries: Argentina, Brazil, Chile, Ecuador, Ghana, Guatemala, India, Ireland, Morocco, Nepal, Nigeria, South Africa, Thailand and Turkey. Most programmes include language training and homestays with families - an excellent way to meet people and learn about local culture.

www.eiluk.org

Frontier Conservation   17+

The Society for Environmental Exploration (SEE), established as a non-profit conservation non-governmental organisation (NGO) dedicated to safeguarding biodiversity and ecosystem integrity, hosts a myriad of global conservation projects under the banner name of Frontier. With a long record of conserving biodiversity, discovering new species, building environmental awareness and developing sustainable livelihoods, Frontier offers 'hands-on' fieldwork, which benefits endangered tropical wildlife and their ecosystems and directly assists developing countries rich in biodiversity but poor in the capacity to manage natural resources.

www.frontier.ac.uk

GAP Activity Projects   17-19

GAP Activity Projects organises voluntary work overseas in over 30 countries. GAP also organises similar exchange voluntary opportunities for overseas nationals in the UK. GAP volunteers work alongside staff in such areas as foreign language assistants, assisting with general activities in schools, caring for the disadvantaged, outdoor education and conservation work. Whatever the nature of your placement, it will always be a challenge. You could be working in an environment different from anything you've ever experienced, so you need to adapt to your responsibilities with maturity. As well as making a real difference to the lives of others, you'll certainly learn a lot about yourself.

www.gap.org.uk

Gapwork   **17+**

Whether it's skiing in the Rocky Mountains, volunteering in a South African safari park or tracking river dolphins in the Amazon that you want, you should find something suitable in the Gapwork activities section. Other sections include jobs, community development, sports and study abroad.

www.gapwork.com

Global Choices   **17+**

Based in London, Global Choices offers programmes classified in five types: Working Holidays, Internships, Teaching Abroad, Volunteering and Courses. Destination countries include Greece, Spain, Ireland, USA, Australia, China, India and Brazil, in addition to the United Kingdom.

www.globalchoices.co.uk

Global Vision International (GVI)   **18+**

GVI is a non-political, non-religious organisation, which through its alliance with over 150 project partners in over 30 countries provides opportunities for volunteers to fill a critical void in the fields of environmental research, conservation, education and community development. International partners include the South African National Parks Board, Diane Fossey Gorilla Fund, Jane Goodall Institute, Rainforest Concern and Kenyan Wildlife Service.

www.gvi.co.uk

Global Volunteer Network   **18+**

This network offers volunteer opportunities in community projects throughout the world, currently providing volunteer programmes through partner organisations in Alaska, Cambodia, China, Costa Rica, Ecuador, El Salvador, Ghana, Honduras, India, Kenya, Nepal, New Zealand, Philippines, Romania, Russia, Rwanda, South Africa, Tanzania, Thailand, Uganda, and Vietnam. The network continues to expand with new programmes continuously being researched and assessed.

www.volunteer.org.nz

Greenforce 17+

Much of Greenforce's current activity is focused on conserving coral reefs. Widely known as the rainforests of the sea, the reefs are home to a massive diversity of species and are much more than just a pretty underwater garden for divers to enjoy. On land, the competition for living space and resources is pushing wildlife into ever shrinking zones. The challenge for conservationists is to resist the pressure to deforest and reap resources in favour of creating protected areas for wildlife and drawing up management plans for sustainable use. A huge part of the work that Greenforce does is also to contribute to improving the lives of fragile and sometimes threatened communities, such as the Maasai in parts of Kenya and Tanzania, and the Quichua Indians deep in the Amazon jungle.

www.greenforce.org

Habitat for Humanity 18+

An international charity working to end poverty housing around the world, Habitat for Humanity works in over 3,000 communities in 92 countries. You would normally spend around two weeks on location in a small community, actually building a house hand–in–hand with a partner family.

www.habitatforhumanity.org.uk

Help2educate 18+

Help2educate is a small registered charity that raises money to fund the education of child labourers in Nepal. It makes it possible to move children from dangerous working conditions and place them in a hostel where they can live and study. Most of the funds are raised by arranging for volunteers to teach in Nepal throughout the year. To teach in a Nepal school or help deprived children in a hostel can be a challenging, adventurous and worthwhile experience for people of any age and background.

www.help2educate.com

i to i   17+

In the past 12 months, i-to-i has: helped 5,000 people volunteer for projects in 23 countries; trained 15,000 people to Teach English as a Foreign Language (TEFL) and assisted them in finding jobs in Cambodia, China, France, Greece, Italy, Japan, Korea, Mexico, Nepal, Poland and Spain; and raised US$130,000 through its charity arm, the i-to-i Foundation, to buy much-needed materials for vital projects around the world.

www.i-to-i.com

International Voluntary Service (IVS GB)   18+

A peace organisation working for the sustainable development of local and global communities throughout the world, IVS GB is the British contact for Service Civil International, a worldwide network of like-minded voluntary organisations promoting peace and justice through voluntary work. By taking part in an International Voluntary Project, you will be working and living alongside other volunteers from all over the world and contributing to local community development. There are hundreds of projects to choose from, including environmental conservation on beaches in Morocco, help at a centre for children with disabilities in Latvia, work with elderly people in mountain villages in Japan, a community theatre in the Czech Republic, and youth work in Russia.

www.ivs-gb.org.uk

Kibbutz Representatives   18-35

Living and working in a kibbutz community in Israel, carrying out the true principles of a socialistic society, having all work, property and profit equally shared by its members, can form the basis of an intriguing working holiday experience. A holiday with the possibility to meet, live and work with both Israeli youngsters and other kibbutz volunteers from countries and cultures from far and near.

www.kibbutz.org.il/eng/welcome.htm

Lean on Me

Aiming to improve the lives of people infected with or affected by HIV/AIDS, the Lean on Me organisers encourage volunteers to return to their countries as ambassadors for AIDS awareness and the hardships Africans face.

www.wecare4africa.com

Learn Overseas   17+

Specialists in India, Learn Overseas offer work experience placements, gap year programmes, career breaks, community based projects and professionally led expeditions, mainly in and around Delhi.

www.learnoverseas.co.uk

Millennium Volunteers   16-25

Millennium Volunteers (MVs) are young people who give up their free time to help their local communities. You might find them coaching a school football team, working at a community radio station or helping create a garden for local residents. Through the course of their voluntary work, MVs gain valuable skills and experience that they can make use of in the workplace, such as team working, decision making and communication. MVs can learn practical skills too, such as designing websites or cooking. Having MV on your CV is something that can make employers and universities sit up and take notice. If you are aged between 16 and 24, Millennium Volunteers could be for you. MV is a national movement with 130 projects established around England, mostly based in local volunteering centres, schools or colleges.

www.millenniumvolunteers.gov.uk

National Trust

If you don't want to travel too far but are still looking for a way to make a difference in conserving the environment and the UK's heritage, the National Trust could have something to offer. As a volunteer, you can learn new skills and meet new people while working right at the heart of beautiful buildings, gardens and landscapes. The Trust also runs around 450 Working Holidays every year throughout England, Wales and Northern Ireland, where you could be involved with anything from carrying out a conservation survey to herding goats, painting a lighthouse or planting trees.

www.nationaltrust.org.uk/volunteering

Outreach International   17+

This specialist organisation has a wide variety of projects, all of them small, grassroots initiatives working with communities where volunteer work can make a big difference. There are one-month and three- to twelve-month projects in countries including Cambodia, Costa Rica, Ecuador, Galapagos Islands, Mexico and Sri Lanka.

www.outreachinternational.co.uk

Oyster Worldwide   18+

Oyster offers projects working with children and teaching English in Brazil, Chilean Patagonia, Kenya, Nepal, Romania and Tanzania. Pre-departure training is included, as well as appropriate language training on arrival. The company also has some paid work opportunities in hotels and ski resorts in the Canadian Rockies and Quebec.

www.oysterworldwide.com

Personal Overseas Development (PoD)   17+

PoD provides the opportunity for you to volunteer and make a difference in parts of the world that are rich in culture, variety and natural beauty but where there is poverty or disadvantage. You may be on your gap year or wanting to volunteer as part of a working holiday abroad. Projects are currently available in Peru, Tanzania, Nepal and Thailand.

www.thepodsite.co.uk

PGL Travel   18+

PGL provides children's adventure holidays at its 33 activity centres across the UK, France and Spain. Every year it recruits over 2,500 staff to instruct, inspire and look after its guests, with vacancies for watersports instructors, adventure activity instructors, group leaders, language speakers, administrators, and maintenance, catering and domestic staff. There are also ad hoc ski rep positions are for the peak weeks of the winter operating season.

www.pgl.co.uk/people

Prince's Trust Volunteers   14-30

The Prince's Trust helps young people overcome barriers and get their lives working. Through practical support including training, mentoring and financial assistance, the Trust helps 14-30 year olds realise their potential and transform their lives. The main target groups are those who have struggled at school, been in care, been in trouble with the law, or are long-term unemployed. As a volunteer with the Trust, you could have a powerful influence on the success of its programmes, and on the young people they help.

www.princes-trust.org.uk

Project Trust   17+

Based on the Isle of Coll, Project Trust specialises in year-long programmes rather than brief visits. You can choose from over 20 different countries, spending a year living, working and travelling outside Europe with a wide variety of work and a diverse range of cultures.

www.projecttrust.org.uk

REACH

Not aimed primarily at school or college leavers, REACH seeks to match the skills of experienced people to the needs of voluntary organisations. REACH recruits and supports people with managerial, technical and professional expertise and places them in part-time, unpaid roles in voluntary organisations that need their help. Volunteers are placed with organisations near where they live, anywhere in the UK.

www.volwork.org.uk

Students Partnership Worldwide   18-28

If you are passionate about changing lives and want to make a difference to the community that you work with, you can volunteer to work for five to eleven months in India, Zambia, Uganda, Tanzania, South Africa or Nepal. You might find yourself helping vulnerable young people protect themselves against HIV, open a library or a youth centre, construct a smokeless stove or establish a recycling programme.

www.spw.org

Teaching and Projects Abroad   17+

With a very wide range of projects, including teaching, care, conservation, medicine and journalism, Teaching and Projects Abroad organises overseas voluntary work placements designed specifically for the communities where it works. The teaching projects focus on conversational English teaching and don't require TEFL qualifications. You could teach in Africa, Asia, Latin America or Eastern Europe, as part of a project in a school, university or orphanage. Teaching volunteers also often help with other activities, such as sport, music or drama for example. In journalism, you could work on a Chinese, Indian, Ghanaian, Mexican, Moldovan, Mongolian, Romanian or Sri Lankan newspaper or work at a radio station in Ghana, Senegal or Mexico or even a TV station in Mongolia.

www.teaching-abroad.co.uk

Travellers Worldwide   17+

Offering a variety of projects lasting from two weeks to a year, Travellers Worldwide seeks to help children, adults, animals and entire communities in less advantaged countries. The only qualifications you need are a spirit of adventure and a sense of humour.

www.travellersworldwide.com

Visit Oz   17-30

If you are considering a gap year in Australia before you go to university, after you have graduated or at any time before your 31st birthday, Visitoz guarantees to find you a job on the land or in rural hospitality, as well as providing agricultural or hospitality training. You must have a Working Holiday Visa (or other Visa allowing work) and be prepared to get your hands dirty. Outback farm or station work can include working with horses, cattle and sheep, tractor and header driving, bulldozer work, fencing, mechanical work, and chainsaw work; horse work may be at stables, in trail riding centres, on Host Farms, with racehorses, polo ponies, camp draft horses or on cattle properties doing bore running, yard work, and maintenance; agricultural bike work is with cattle and sheep. There are so many jobs that it is possible to find something to suit the skills of everybody.

www.visitoz.org

Voluntary Service Overseas   18+

VSO has programmes and volunteers in 34 countries around the world. It offers a Youth Volunteering programme for young people aged 18 to 25, although its main volunteers are aged from 20 to 75 and must have a formal qualification and relevant work experience. Regular postings are for two years and volunteers are provided with accommodation and a local level allowance as well as air fares and insurance.

www.vso.org.uk

Volunteering England

Volunteering England works to support an increase in the quality, quantity, impact and accessibility of volunteering throughout England. You can volunteer for a very wide range of activities. From helping an elderly neighbour with their shopping to providing legal advice for a local charity, volunteers make a vital contribution to all aspects of community life.

www.volunteering.org.uk

Winant Clayton Volunteer Association   18+

WCVA has over 50 years' experience placing volunteers in community projects in the United States. You could work with children, the elderly, the homeless, adults with mental health problems and many more. Previous experience is valuable but not essential. You will get direct experience of being part of a local community project in the United States. The work will be challenging and you will discover skills, potential and strengths that you never knew you had.

www.wcva.dircon.co.uk

Wind, Sand and Stars - Sinai Summer Expedition   16-23

The Summer Expedition is a three-week journey through the Sinai with the local Bedouin. It combines trekking in the high mountain region, learning about team management and survival, with working on community based projects for the Bedouin. The Expedition runs from mid July to mid August and is open to students aged between 16 and 23. During the expedition you will work on a local Garden Regeneration project alongside the local Bedouin tribes within a mountain area. The projects are chosen in conjunction with the Bedouin and designed to ensure that they meet a very real need.

www.windsandstars.co.uk

Worldwide Volunteering   16+

This organisation offers a 'search and match' database with over 1300 volunteer organisations and 350,000 placements throughout the UK and in 214 countries worldwide.

www.wwv.org.uk

Year Out Group   17+

Formed in 1998 to promote the concept and benefits of well-structured year out programmes, to promote models of good practice and to help young people and their advisers in selecting suitable and worthwhile projects, Year Out Group is a not-for-profit association of UK registered organisations that specialise in this field. All the member organisations are carefully vetted on joining and provide annual confirmation that they continue to abide by the Group's Code of Practice and Operating Guidelines.

www.yearoutgroup.org

Treks/Expeditions and Activity Holidays

If you want to combine an adventure trek with an environmental, scientific or community project, you may find something suitable here. Expect to pay a substantial participation fee, for which you may have to raise sponsorship. Apart from being one of the best ways in which to fund your expedition, the experience of having to secure a considerable sum of money will help develop a range of skills before you even leave home! Expedition programmes give you the opportunity to develop many other important skills such as communication and time management. You'll be building confidence and self-esteem, in addition to learning to lead an expedition team and taking your turn to do so. You should also meet a group of like-minded people and have a lot of fun. Whatever destination you choose, you could end up doing something that will look good on your CV and will be highly valued by universities and employers.

BSES Expeditions 16+

The British Schools Exploring Society organises extreme adventure and conservation expeditions in remote, wild environments. You could find yourself monitoring climate change in the Arctic, measuring biodiversity in the jungle or investigating human impact on the environment in mountainous regions. The aim is always to develop the confidence, teamwork, leadership and spirit of adventure and exploration of all expedition members.

www.bses.org.uk

GAP/World Challenge Expeditions 17-24

On a World Challenge overseas expedition, you could soon be trekking through the jungles of Borneo or climbing Mount Kenya. Many expeditions are organised for school groups but you can participate as an individual. There are one-month expeditions suitable for young people up to the age of 22, with destinations including the Andes and Amazon (Peru), Borneo, Central America (Belize, Mexico and Guatemala), East Africa (Kenya), and India and Himalaya.

www.world-challenge.co.uk

Jubilee Sailing Trust 16+

The Jubilee Sailing Trust (JST) is a charity that aims to promote the integration of people of all physical abilities through the challenge and adventure of tall ship sailing. The JST owns and operates two tall ships - LORD NELSON and TENACIOUS - the only two vessels in the world that have been purpose-designed and built to enable a crew of mixed physical abilities to sail side by side on equal terms. If you take on the tall ship challenge with the JST, it could be a short hop around the British coast, a four-week transatlantic challenge, a week's island hopping in the Canary Islands or the Caribbean, or a place in the European Tall Ships' Race

www.jst.org.uk

Madventurer and Sportventurer 17+

As a volunteer, you become part of the Mad Tribe. The spirit of volunteering brings together all shapes and sizes and accents. Each year there is a Mad World Ball in Newcastle upon Tyne, for reunions and reminiscing of the time you've weathered and treasured together. Madventurer rural projects focus on building basic infrastructure to assist local community development. The key focus is youth development and the provision and improvement of health, education and sanitation facilities such as schools, clinics, toilets, water storage tanks, community centres and sanitation facilities. Venturers also have the opportunity to teach English and other subjects in local primary schools, as well as getting involved in extracurricular activities such as sports, art and drama.

www.madventurer.com

Outward Bound Trust 11 to 17+

Outward Bound seek to help young people have access to safe, adventurous experiences - from abseiling to zip wiring - through which you can raise your self-esteem, realise your full potential and achieve more than you ever thought possible. Among the 'Ultimate adventures for individuals' are UK expeditions in the Scottish Highlands, the Isle of Skye and Wales and global expeditions in Transylvania (Romania), Sabah (Malaysia), and South Africa.

www.outwardbound-uk.org

Quest Overseas 17+

Specialists in Africa and South America, Quest offer 'Combined Gap Expeditions', in which you can learn a language, work on a community or conservation project and then explore the best of the surrounding countries. This could lead, for example, to Community Development work in Tanzania or a Game Reserve project in Swaziland, together with exploration of southern Africa, or an Animal Sanctuary project in Bolivia, together with exploration of the Andes.

www.questoverseas.com

Raleigh International   17+

The Raleigh overseas programme enables participants aged 17 to 24 from all over the world and from all backgrounds to undertake a blend of mental and physical challenges. The full 10-week programme consists of three distinct project phases - sustainable community and environmental projects plus an adventure phase. There are also five-week programmes, which combine your choice of either a community or environmental project with a team-based adventure challenge. Destinations include Costa Rica & Nicaragua, Namibia and Malaysia (Borneo).

www.raleigh.org.uk

Tall Ships Youth Trust   16+

The Tall Ships Youth Trust owns two 60 metre square-rigged ships. They are operated by Tall Ships Ltd., one of the charity's subsidiaries, and work 12 months of the year both around the UK and abroad, offering Tall Ship Adventure Sailing Holidays.

www.tallships.org

The Leap Overseas   17+

The Leap offers adventurous team or solo voluntary work placements in Africa, South America, Asia and Australia. All placements combine conservation, eco-tourism and community projects, otherwise known as the Three Leaps. This mix of challenges and experiences, combined with adventure travel in the form of scuba diving, kite surfing, white water rafting, riding or polo, should serve to broaden your horizons and surpass your expectations.

www.theleap.co.uk

Trekforce Expeditions   18+

With over 20 years' experience of organising expeditions - that combine real adventure with a serious purpose - in the rainforests, deserts and mountains of the world, Trekforce Worldwide run one-to five-month expeditions and gap year programmes that tackle tough conservation or development projects, and can be followed by intensive language courses and long-term teaching placements in rural communities. They also offer a series of two-to three-week Extreme Expeditions to the most testing environments around the world, designed to push you to the very limit.

www.trekforce.org.uk

Ventureco   17+

VentureCo's multi-phase travel programmes incorporate development projects, expeditions and adventure travel in Asia, Africa, South America and Central America. The ventures are a combination of complementary phases. For example, in South America you would combine a Spanish language phase with a Project phase and an Expedition phase to make one venture. Each phase reveals a different aspect of your host country and together they produce one memorable travel experience.

Participation in the venture is the most important element of its success: venturers are team players with considerable input into the everyday running of each phase. Venturers are aged between 17 and 20 and applications are taken from the UK and overseas.

www.ventureco-worldwide.com

Woodlarks Campsite Trust, Surrey   16+

Situated in twelve acres of beautiful Surrey countryside, Woodlarks Campsite enables children and adults with disabilities to enjoy a host of activities they may never have thought possible.

Woodlarks camps can be as tranquil or as adventurous as you want them to be.

www.woodlarks.org.uk

Learn how business works…and get paid for it in some cases! You may be carrying out research, designing prototypes, planning projects, handling customers' needs or devising new working methods. Projects vary depending on company needs.

BBC

The British Broadcasting Corporation has work experience placements available in just about every area of BBC activity across the UK. Whatever your age and whichever area you're interested in, there could be something right for you, from advertising, charitable work or entertaining to journalism, music or the World Service. All placements are unpaid and can last anything from a few days to four weeks. Competition is fierce, so before you apply you'll need to consider what you can offer and what you'd like to achieve. Are you good with computers? Have you worked in hospital radio or written articles for your local or college magazine? What do you hope to gain from the placement? What are your ambitions for the future? These are the kind of questions you should be asking yourself.

www.bbc.co.uk/jobs/workexperience

BigWee   14-19

The Big Work Experience Exchange invites parents who can offer work experience placements to register them online, with the aim of exchanging opportunities with like-minded people. As a member, you can search the database in the hope of finding a placement to meet your own needs and, on payment of a fee, will have access to the complete list of opportunities available including all contact details.

www.bigwee.com

Engineering Education Scheme (England)   16-17+

This programme links teams of four Year 12 students and your teacher with local companies to work on real scientific, engineering and technological problems.

www.thescheme.org.uk

John Lewis Partnership   16-17+

Students gain an opportunity to spend two weeks in a department store, where they can gain an insight into the world of retailing. Placements normally take place in selling departments but we will try to accommodate students in other areas of the business if they have a particular interest. Students fill in an application form and have a brief interview – as they would if they were applying for a real job. We prefer schools to apply on behalf of their students but we will accept individual enquiries. Schools should apply to their local department store.

www.johnlewispartnership.co.uk

PricewaterhouseCoopers   17+

Running from September to March each year, the PwC Gap Year Programme offers a lucrative way of taking some time out between leaving school or college and going to university. You can pick up some worthwhile experience - and cash - along the way. The Gap Year Programme is about getting hands-on experience in the world's largest professional services firm: for seven months you will effectively be working for PwC full time and contributing to real client projects. The nature of your work will depend on the vacancy you fill, which in turn depends on which area of business you're interested in. There are vacancies each year within Assurance, Tax, Forensic Services and the Actuarial team.

www.pwc.com/uk/eng/car-inexp/tg/gap.html

Smallpeice Trust   18+

The Trust offers four-day residential courses at universities, allowing you to develop your interest in engineering by exploring specific areas such as aerospace or supercomputing in engineering, placing you alongside real engineers, professionals and technical specialists.

www.smallpeicetrust.org.uk

The Trident Trust   14-25

Helps 14-25 year olds to prepare for life beyond the classroom by finding them work experience opportunities and running a 'skills for life' course. The Trident Trust helps young people improve their employability and enterprise skills and develop as individuals.

www.thetridenttrust.org.uk

Year in Industry 17+

The Year in Industry scheme offers paid, degree relevant work placements in a year out before or during your university course. With opportunities in all branches of engineering, science, computing and business management, you can undertake real projects and learn how business works. The skills you develop should enhance your university education and maximise your graduate job prospects. Many companies view the scheme as an important part of their recruitment programme, and go on to sponsor placement students through university.

www.yini.org.uk

Science and Engineering

The rapid expansion of new ideas springing from these fields is transforming our economic prospects and competitiveness in global markets. The enthusiasm of scientists and engineers has never been greater as they see their fields open rapidly into highly successful world wide companies. You could catch much of their excitement and motivation in many of these opportunities.

The British Association for the Advancement of Science
14-19

The British Association for the Advancement of Science organises National Science Week in March with over 2,000 scientific, engineering and technology events occurring throughout the country and the Festival of Science in September which includes dialogue events for 14-19 yr olds. Information is sent direct to schools.

www.the-ba.net

Embryo Veterinary School, Devon 17+

The Embryo team of experienced vets and academics offer a three-day course for aspiring vets, giving detailed analysis of Veterinary Science degree courses, and honest insight into the realities of the job. Set in rural Devon, the course provides an opportunity to spend time in a working veterinary practice environment.

www.embryoveterinaryschool.com

Engineering Education Scheme in England 16+

The scheme, sponsored by the Royal Academy of Engineering, aims to help young people achieve their full potential in engineering, science and technology. Students are given the opportunity to work in an engineering environment for a few months before taking A levels.

www.thescheme.org.uk

Headstart Courses 16+

A well-established education programme whose aim is to encourage students interested in mathematics or science to consider technology-based careers. It provides an opportunity for you in Year 12/S5 to spend up to a week at university prior to making your UCAS application.

Headstart courses are divided into four distinct categories: Engineering (broad-based), Focus (single discipline), Insight (girls only), and Science and Society.

You have to pay to attend, typically around £185. This includes all accommodation and meals during the course, but not travel costs to and from the university. Some bursaries are available where financial hardship would prevent attendance, and your school may help with the course fee.

www.headstartcourses.org.uk

INSIGHT Courses   16+

INSIGHT Courses are for the young woman with a genuine interest in becoming an engineer. Applicants spend a week at university living in student residences. You will have opportunities to find out about different fields of engineering, spend a day with an engineering company and meet other women who are working successfully in engineering and technology based careers.

www.enginuity.org.uk

The Royal Institution of Great Britain   All ages

An important part of the work of the Royal Institution is to promote an understanding of science in young people. To further this aim, lectures and events are held throughout the year specifically targeted at the new generation of budding scientists. The lectures for young people are held during the Christmas holidays.

www.rigb.org

Salters' Chemistry Camps   14-16

Hugely popular four-day residential camps for 50 15 year-olds at universities throughout the UK, packed with exciting chemistry and social events. The aim of the camps is to encourage young people to participate in the fun of chemistry and motivate them to develop awareness of and a long term interest in the subject.

www.salters.co.uk/camps

Salters' Festivals of Chemistry   11-13

The Festivals are one-day events for schools held at universities throughout the UK and Ireland. Competing schools are represented by a team of four students from years 7 or 8 where they take part in two, hands-on, practical activities followed by fun lecturing and prizegiving. No prior preparation required.

www.salters.co.uk/festivals

The Workshop, Loughborough   17+

The Workshop offers 2- and 3-day courses covering various degree course subjects including business, law, nursing, medicine, veterinary medicine, physiotherapy and psychology.

www.workshop-uk.com

Business Skills

Aquiring these modern business skills, learning to use computers and, software, spreadsheets, packages, can greatly enhance your effectiveness in higher education for all academic subjects, for research and essay projects, for dissertations, data handling and retrieval. These skills, if fully developed can greatly improve your eventual job prospects, and value to employers.

Oxford Media and Business School   17+

The School's 'Gap Year Life Skills' course is designed to give you an early taste of a university style environment, together with training in key Life Skills such as the use of the latest IT software. The Careers Direct placement bureau will then help you find temping work, which can be invaluable both for later university submissions and for earning cash to fund the rest of your Gap Year.

www.oxfordbusiness.co.uk

Pitman Training 17+

There are more than 90 Pitman Training Centres all over the UK, Ireland and the Middle East, training 50,000 people every year. Courses are available in areas such as IT and Business skills, including Bookkeeping and Accounts, Web Design, Shorthand, Spreadsheets and Word Processing.

www.pitman-training.com

Queen's Business and Secretarial College, London 16+

The six-week Business Skills Course at Queen's is popular with gap-year students and graduates who are in a hurry to gain skills and move into the workplace. There is also a one-term Intensive Course offering a choice between learning shorthand or extra IT skills with an external qualification. Other courses include the three-term Marketing and Business Skills course and the two-term Executive and Personal Assistant's course.

www.qbsc.ac.uk

St James's and Lucie Clayton College, London 15+

The founding philosophy of St. James's and Lucie Clayton College is to deliver essential business skills to enhance the career prospects of all of its students. Recognising that academic qualifications, regardless of grades or levels, may not always secure good employment prospects, the College focuses on skills such as good touch typing, the ability to produce commercial letters and documents, and a sound knowledge of IT, the internet & email. Personal development modules ensure that confidence and style are included alongside the acquisition of interview techniques and effective communication skills.

www.sjlccollege.co.uk

Workshop Conferences 17+

The Workshop offers two- and three-day residential conferences at the University of Nottingham, covering such career/degree-related topics as: business and management, criminal law, nursing, medicine, physiotherapy, psychology, veterinary science and working with animals.

www.workshop-uk.com

Sports Related

Whether you are new to a sport or already experienced, these courses can enhance your performance. Achieving instructor status could provide opportunities to teach a sport to fellow undergraduates and to represent your university in eg golf, tennis, sailing, rowing, football.

David Lloyd Leisure   15+

With 59 clubs across the UK, David Lloyd Leisure could help you improve your health and fitness. The group's racquets facilities include 500 tennis courts (over half of which are indoor), 100 badminton courts and 85 squash courts.

www.davidlloydleisure.co.uk

Exsportise 9-16

Coaching in tennis, field hockey, golf and football. Residential and day courses for all abilities. Activities occur during Christmas, Easter and the summer holidays. Locations: Seaford College, Sussex and Clayesmore School, Dorset.

www.exsportise.co.uk

Flying Fish 17+

This organisation offers professional training for yachtmasters and instructors in yachting, dinghy sailing, windsurfing, surfing, diving, snowboarding and skiing. As an experienced yacht skipper or instructor, you can then spend time earning money from your favourite sport.

www.flyingfishonline.com

The International Academy 16+

The International Academy provides instructor training courses in skiing, snowboarding, scuba diving and flying. The ski and snowboard instructor training courses are run in partnership with the resident ski and snowboard schools in ski resorts including Whistler Blackcomb and Lake Louise. Scuba diving instructor training courses are run through specialist centres in Egypt, Cyprus and Malta, providing the opportunity for you to gain PADI Divemaster or Instructor qualifications. You can also learn how to fly an aeroplane or helicopter in Florida and gain a JAA or FAA Private Pilot Licence.

www.international-academy.com

Jonathan Markson Tennis 10+

A graduate of Christ Church College, Oxford, Jonathan Markson is a former captain and coach of the Oxford University 'blues' tennis team and an international player for Scotland. His company offers tennis holidays and tennis camps in England, Portugal, Spain, Italy, Cyprus, South Africa, Tunisia, Czech Republic, Hungary and the USA.

www.marksontennis.com

NONSTOP Ski   17+

This company provides a range of ski instructor courses and improvement camps in the Canadian Rockies, renowned for their abundant snowfall and world class skiing. Courses are based in Fernie, Banff, Whistler and Red Mountain. The intensive 11-week courses provide the chance to master your skiing whilst opening up work opportunities within the ski industry. Extended stays are available, allowing you to spend up to six months in Canada.

www.nonstopski.com

Peak Leaders   17+

Peak Leaders' Ski and Snowboard courses ensure you will be improving your technical skills, gaining snowsports qualifications, and increasing your understanding of mountain environments, safety and team leading. At the same time, you'll be experiencing life in another culture such as in Canada, New Zealand, South America, France or Switzerland. There are also nine-week summer break, southern hemisphere courses, with the emphasis on travel and adventure.

www.peakleaders.com

Windmill Hill Tennis and Golf Academy, East Sussex   15+

Catering for players of all ages and abilities, from absolute beginners to experienced competitors, Windmill Hill Tennis and Golf Academy offers coaching holidays the whole year round. The programme includes tuition and video analysis each full day, in classes of no more than 8 to 10 players.

www.windmillhill.co.uk

See Also

Language Skills

These organisations offer a chance to improve your chosen languages, to travel widely abroad, to experience the cultures, politics, and economics of other countries. If you are intending to study languages, geography, international business or law - very valuable background can be gained- and many other opportunities can be opened up for your university vacations and future career outlook.

Dragons International   11-19

Dragons International are specialists in the organisation of travel for school groups within Europe. Dragons offers a door-to-door service and are a fully bonded tour operator of the Association of British Travel Agents. Group bookings only.

http://www.dragonsinternational.co.uk

Languages Abroad - CESA   16+

A Languages for Life courses immerses you in a language, teaches you key language skills and provides you with the opportunities to put these skills into daily practice. You will gain a wider and richer knowledge of the vocabulary, grammar and syntax of the language or, at a higher ability level, you can add layers of understanding in the form of +nuance and cultural reference critical to real language competence. Students of European languages can see tangible results over an 8- to 16-week period, although you can study for longer. If studying Arabic or Russian, you may need 8 to 20 weeks for serious linguistic improvement, and 12 to 24 weeks for Japanese or Chinese.

http://www.cesalanguages.com/

Rotary International Youth Exchange   16+

Each year the Rotary Youth Exchange programme sends literally thousands of young people, aged up to 25 years of age, on long- and short-term exchanges, special interest camps and tours. These aim to promote an insight into another country's way of life, traditions, culture and develop lasting friendships.

www.youthribi.org

Drama and Music

These superb events are available for students who are keen to gain greater experience of drama and music. They provide exceptionally valuable background awareness and an opportunity to share the enthusiasm and creativity of others, and to greatly improve their skills.

European Union Youth Orchestra   14-24

The Orchestra is made up of some 120 players, representing all 27 member countries of the European Union (EU). The players are selected each year from over 4,000 candidates aged up to 24, who take part in auditions throughout the EU. Once the members have been selected for the year, you are invited to join the Orchestra to rehearse and perform major works on international stages all over the world. There are two rounds of auditions in the UK and Ireland: Preliminaries are held in Birmingham, Cork, Dublin, Glasgow, London and Manchester; Finals are held in London and Dublin.

www.euyo.org.uk

National Association of Youth Theatres   14 to adult

The Association supports the development of youth theatre activity through training, advocacy, participation programmes and information services. Its Big Youth Theatre Festival is an outdoor event including opportunities to perform, take part in a wide range of workshops, see others perform and meet youth theatre members from other countries.

www.nayt.org.uk

National Student Drama Festival, Scarborough   16+

The springtime Festival is a week-long celebration of theatre, live performance, discussion and special events. You can attend workshops and debates covering all aspects of theatre and performance, including acting, dance, writing, directing, designing, devising and producing. Practitioners come from all over the world and there are opportunities to take part in performances, even if you are not part of a selected show.

www.nsdf.org.uk

National Youth Orchestra   13-19

One of the world's finest youth orchestras, the National Youth Orchestra (NYO) draws together each year over 150 talented musicians, aged up to 19, from all over the UK. The orchestra meets during the school holidays at New Year, Easter and Summer for intensive two-week periods of coaching and rehearsal with NYO Professors - leading professional musicians and teachers - and some of the world's finest conductors and soloists.

www.nyo.org.uk

National Youth Orchestras of Scotland   **12-21**

The National Youth Orchestras of Scotland (NYOS) provides top-class music education and performance experience for young musicians (up to the age of 221) throughout Scotland. Running six national youth ensembles, NYOS organises training, intensive rehearsals and national and international concert tours. As well as running the six orchestras, NYOS is committed to introducing musical experiences to all of Scotland's young people.

www.nyos.co.uk

Year Out Drama   **18+**

This is a full-time programme providing an intensive practical drama course with a theatre company feel. The course includes Acting, Directing, Design, Costume, Voice Work, Movement, Text Study, Theatre Trips and at least four full-scale performances during the year, including a production at the Edinburgh Fringe.

www.yearoutdrama.com

Art and Design

These courses speak for themselves. The Art History Abroad course offers a superb opportunity to study Italian art and architecture. This would provide a foundation for degree courses in art or architectural history. Other valuable taster courses in art and design and related areas are available in the UK, at universities and colleges. These are indexed on page 84.

Art History Abroad 16/17+

AHA's six-week course involves travelling throughout Italy to study at first hand many masterpieces of Italian art. The programme includes visits to Venice (10 nights), Verona (4 nights), Florence (10 nights), Siena (4 nights), Naples (4 nights) and Rome (10 nights), together with day excursions to at least six of: Padua, Vicenza, Ravenna, Modena, Urbino, Pisa, San Gimignano, Arezzon, Orvieto, Pompeii and Tivoli.

www.arthistoryabroad.com

JJA Academy for Art and Design Appreciation, London 21+

The Academy's most comprehensive and sought after course is its Diploma in Art and Design, comprising 100 days taken full-time over a 6, 9 or 12 month flexible period to suit your own needs and timetable.

www.academyforartdesign.co.uk

KLC School of Design, London 18+

The one-week Introduction to Interior Decoration at the KLC Studio in Chelsea gives an insight into the whole process of interior design. The approach is practical with a combination of lectures and workshops with advice on how to plan a room layout and how to create a cohesive interior style by developing ideas from a basic concept. Also popular is the one-week Introduction to Garden Design.

www.klc.co.uk

Cookery Skills

Some course listed here could help you decide whether you would like to train for a career as a professional cook; others can lead to gap-year employment as a chalet cook; others are specifically geared to help future university students prepare simple meals for survival on something more than beans on toast after leaving home.

Ballymaloe Cookery School, Ireland   16+

Run by Ireland's most famous TV cook Darina Allen, Ballymaloe offers a highly regarded 12-week certificate course, graduates of which are in demand all over the world. There is also a wide range of shorter courses - some suitable for complete beginners, others aimed at more experienced cooks. A special time every day is lunch, when teachers and students sit down together to enjoy a three-course meal, which the students have prepared using recipes from the demonstrations.

www.cookingisfun.ie

Cookie Crumbles, London   15+

Although Cookie Crumbles specialises in fun cookery for younger children, there are occasional workshops for school and college leavers, giving a firm grasp of how to eat well when cooking for yourself in a hall of residence or in a student house.

www.cookiecrumbles.net

Edinburgh School of Food and Wine   16+

Among a wide range of courses, you may be particularly interested in the Edinburgh School's four-week intensive certificate course, designed to help you earn your keep during a gap year. This practical course will give you the fundamental skills needed to cook for, say, a ski chalet or a highland lodge and a grounding in cookery for life. Also highly relevant is the one-week 'survival course', designed to develop your culinary talents through a combination of demonstration and practical sessions.

www.esfw.com

Le Cordon Bleu   18+

You might try the four-week 'Taste of Healthy Eating' course at this world-renowned institute's London School, or you could consider a short course at one of its centres in France, Canada, Japan, Australia, Mexico or South Korea.

www.cordonbleu.edu

Leith's School of Food and Wine, London   17+

The School offers a varied menu of courses for professional cooks and enthusiastic amateurs. Especially relevant for readers of this book is the one-week 'Survival Cooking' course. This is aimed at those leaving home or cooking on their own for the first time and wishing to equip themselves with basic skills and recipes to allow them to cook nutritionally balanced food on a budget. The course also looks at how to make very simple dishes look impressive, and at how humble ingredients can make delicious meals.

www.leiths.com

Nairn's Cook School, Scotland   16+

TV chef Nick Nairn runs one- and five-day master classes in the building blocks of cooking, covering the five key areas of the kitchen in great depth. You can spend a full week at the school or a day here and there - there's no obligation to carry out all the subjects in one block. The School is hidden away in the foothills of the Trossachs, right at the heart of some of Scotland's finest scenery, yet less than an hour away from Edinburgh or Glasgow.

www.nicknairncookschool.com

The Orchards School of Cookery, Worcestershire   16+

The one- and two-week 'Chalet Cook' courses can show you how to master the art of being a great chalet cook, enabling you to get the most out of a gap-year job in the mountains. Alternatively, the five-day 'Off to University' course covers healthy, delicious and affordable meals for students, including easy entertaining.

www.orchardscookery.co.uk

Padstow Seafood School, Cornwall   8-14

TV chef Rick Stein's famous cooking school mostly caters for adults, but does offer half-day courses for students during the Easter and summer holidays.

www.rickstein.com

Tante Marie School of Cookery, Surrey   16+

Renowned for its professional Diploma courses, Tante Marie offers three shorter courses particularly suited to readers of this book. Whether you are keen to go for a gap year job in a stunning location, would like to take your culinary skills to a higher level or just want a short introduction to cooking well for yourself, family and friends, there could be a suitable course for you. The 11-week 'Cordon Bleu Certificate' is highly valued by ski companies and other gap year employers, although you might also consider the four-week 'Essential Skills' course. If you simply want to eat well at university, look at the one- or two-week 'Beginners' courses, offering an introduction to good food and healthy eating.

www.tantemarie.co.uk

Fundraising

We mention at several points in this publication that it will cost you a fairly considerable sum - often several thousand pounds - to participate in some of the projects listed. This is particularly true of many of the international community, environmental or scientific projects.

For example, to go overseas with Project Trust in 2008/9, you will be expected to raise £4480, including deposits of £220. Project Trust will raise another £500 approximately on your behalf to subsidise the full costs of your year abroad.

Organisations such as Project Trust receive no government assistance and all funds must be raised either by project managers or by volunteers like you.

Given that the aim of this book is to provide you with ideas to help develop your personal, learning and thinking skills, we believe that raising sponsorship can be an important part of this process. It shows others your determination and initiative, and it will help you establish in your own mind just how well you can respond to a challenge. You will have to start by learning how to fundraise and how to make the most of the support available.

Experienced organisers of such projects say that most volunteers are surprised by the response to their efforts and many not only hit their target but actually raise more than the sum required. Only a small number each year have problems and even they can usually be helped to find suitable sponsors.

Should you decide to opt for a project with a sizeable participation fee, you will find that the organisers will normally send you, once accepted, a comprehensive pack containing fundraising ideas and information. In addition, there should be an experienced member of staff able to give you help and advice by email or over the telephone.

The list below should give you a clear idea of the level of fundraising support you should look for when researching a possible project:

- **Advice on fundraising:** does the selection process introduce the idea of fundraising through a seminar or workshop, encouraging you to think about it constructively?

- **Ongoing support:** what mechanism exists for you to keep the organisers informed of your progress? If you are struggling, do they provide practical advice?

- **Fundraising meetings:** will you be invited to one or more fundraising meetings, where you can get together with fellow volunteers to share ideas and experiences?

- **Bulletin board:** is there a website bulletin board allowing you and your fellow volunteers to keep in touch?

Fundraising ideas

The best starting point is always to look inside yourself! There should be no need to turn your life around completely to raise the required funds. Consider what you are already good at and love doing, then think about how you can use your skills to make the money you will need.

If you are good at music, for example, you could try your hand at busking, performing at various events or offering home tuition.

If your interests are more sporting, you could arrange a tournament where teams pay to enter and you provide the service of organising it and setting up suitable prizes.

If you can cook, you could offer a catering service for dinner parties and other social gatherings.

If you are green-fingered, you could offer a gardening service or bring on seeds and cuttings to sell at every opportunity.

If none of these applies, you could simply get a part-time job of any sort and start saving regularly to establish your fund. You should, of course, volunteer for every possible additional shift to boost your income!

Once you have a service to offer, goods to sell or a job to find, turn first to your immediate circle of family, friends and school, college or other social contacts, perhaps in a youth or sports club. If they can't offer you direct support, ask them to think about who they could put you in touch with, or who they might be prepared to approach on your behalf. Before long, you should have a long list of potential customers/employers/sponsors!

While you are raising money, don't forget that you will have other things to buy. You might, for example, need a top quality sleeping bag or rucksack, both of which are likely to be expensive. Baggage insurance is another important extra.

When you go, you will need to take some spending money with you: perhaps around £1,000 for a year-long project, although this can depend upon which country you go to. Even if you can afford it, you shouldn't think of taking so much money overseas that you might be tempted to live and travel in a way that would not sit easily with your role as a volunteer.

Managing Risk

Many of the suggestions in this book contain an element of risk. That is part of their attraction...and you will no doubt see little point in trekking through a jungle or across a mountain range if you are going to be as cosy and safe all the time as you are in an armchair at home. Nevertheless, we could not possibly encourage you to take unnecessary risks and we recommend that you venture overseas only with a reputable organisation with experienced leaders and stringent operating procedures designed to avoid foolhardy misadventure.

We cover a broad range of health safety issues in our brief quiz on pages 56 to 61 and we would ask you to spend some time

reading this section and visiting the recommended websites. Amongst them, the *Know before you go* site managed by the Foreign and Commonwealth Office is absolutely essential.

In addition, we suggest that you use the checklist below when choosing an organisation with which to undertake your trip. This will help to ensure that you are in safe hands and will be travelling responsibly.

- **Crisis Management:** Is there a comprehensive crisis management policy in place? How robust is it and how are staff trained to implement it?

- **UK Support:** Does the organisation maintain a 24-hour emergency telephone line for family and friends in the UK?

- **Insurance:** Does the organisation have a comprehensive company insurance policy with a specialist provider?

- **Leaders:** What is the organisation's recruitment policy in relation to the experience and qualifications of expedition leaders? What knowledge do they have of the countries they work in? Do they have relevant language and first aid skills? Does the Criminal Records Bureau carry out checks of their backgrounds?

- **Risk Assessment:** Do expedition leaders undertake daily monitoring of activities in order to maintain the safety of participants? Are written risk assessments available for consultation? Are participants encouraged to carry out their own risk assessments during an expedition?

- **In-Country Support:** Do leaders have up-to-date contact lists for medical and logistical support in the country you will be visiting?

- **Participant Preparation:** What level of pre-departure training and/or in-country orientation is provided for participants?

- **Equipment:** How often is equipment reviewed and replaced? Is safety equipment provided as standard? Do leaders carry comprehensive first aid kits?

- **Transport:** How do leaders assess in-country transport? Is there a policy regarding the use of public or private transport options? Is road transport undertaken at night?

- **Responsible Travel:** What is the organisation's policy in relation to monitoring and minimising the long-term impact of expeditions such as the one you are considering? Is there a long-term commitment to cultural sensitivity and sustainable development?

- **Financial Transparency:** Can the organisation demonstrate that your financial contributions are spent directly on the project and nowhere else?

- **Feedback:** Is there evidence that feedback from participants and staff is assessed and acted upon where necessary to improve future provision?

A final word. While we have tried our best, as publishers of this book, to ensure that you understand the nature of potential hazards overseas - how to recognise and overcome them - we must stress that you cannot rely totally on us or even on the very best provider of specialist gap year activities. You must use your own common sense and initiative to help you to spend your time as safely as possible.

Researching a Skill and Awareness Opportunity

When you have researched the ideas in this book, complete a worksheet for each project, trip or expedition that interests you. Our 10–point plan will help you focus on finding the right programme to develop your personal learning and thinking skills.

Name of organisation
Type of activity
1. What is it that appeals to me? *(Adventure, travel, helping others, earning money)*
2. Am I eligible? *(Right age, available at the right time)*
3. What exactly will I be doing? *(Choice of projects, working with others, accommodation, food)*
4. How will I benefit from this programme?
5. How will other people benefit from my involvement?

6. How much will it cost? *(Total budget, raising funds, putting down a deposit)*

7. Who will I be signing up with?
(Commercial company, registered charity, reputation, experience, equal opportunities)

8. What do I need to arrange? *(Travel, insurance, health check)*

9. Is there any pre-programme training or briefing?

10. What happens afterwards? *(Debriefing, maintain contact, inform future participants, certificate recording achievements)*

Am I Ready For a Trip Abroad?

If you are planning to travel abroad as part of your personal development, try our brief quiz to see how well prepared you are!

1. **INSURANCE ISSUES**

   (a) I will investigate a range of different types of insurance to cover my travel and placement/project ☐

   (b) I will take out a travel insurance for the journeys to and from my placement/project ☐

   (c) I guess that I'm on our family annual travel insurance and that my parents' insurance policies will cover all eventualities ☐

2. **THE COUNTRY I INTEND TO VISIT**

   (a) I have researched the laws and customs of my planned destination as well as the usual food, currency and weather type research ☐

   (b) I have looked at holiday websites to find out about the country I intend to visit ☐

   (c) I'll pick up everything I need to know just by being in the country for several months ☐

3. **VISAS AND PERMITS**

   (a) I have checked out the necessary visas and work permits for the country I intend to visit ☐

   (b) I will see if I need a visa ☐

   (c) Someone will sort out whatever has to happen about a visa for me ☐

4. **HEALTH**

   (a) I will check with my local surgery to see if I need any special injections or healthcare for the country I am visiting a couple of months before the departure date ☐

   (b) I will ask my mum to take a look on the internet to see if there is anything I need to do about health care arrangements for my visit ☐

   (c) I won't bother to do anything special about healthcare as I am young and healthy ☐

5. **SAFETY**

   (a) I have seriously considered a number of ways of ensuring my safety when I am on my placement and I have discussed safety plans with my family ☐

   (b) I am always careful about my well being and I won't need to do anything extra for my placement ☐

   (c) I have no safety worries and I can look after myself ☐

How did you do?

If you answered (a) to all the questions then you have made a good start. All (b) then you have a bit more work to do. All (c) then you really must do a lot more research.

Points to consider

1. Insurance issues

It'll never happen to me!

It can happen to you; things can go wrong. You could fall ill or have an accident; you could have money or luggage stolen; your visit might be cancelled or cut short through injury or illness; your family may need to fly out to be with you if there is a serious incident. So take out insurance. Make sure it's comprehensive and covers you for medical and repatriation costs as well as any dangerous sports or activities.

If you get injured or ill as a result of drugs or alcohol, your insurance may be invalidated and your travel operator can refuse to fly you home.

2. The country I intend to visit

You must read up on the laws and customs of your chosen destination, to avoid offending people or breaking local laws, however unwittingly. The best starting point for this is the Foreign and Commonwealth Office, with its 'Know before you go' awareness campaign aimed at encouraging British travellers to prepare better before going overseas. Visit the website at: www.fco.gov.uk/knowbeforeyougo or telephone 0845 850 2829.

If you are thinking about taking drugs whilst on holiday abroad or bringing some back with you, stop and think - otherwise your trip of a lifetime could end up lasting a lifetime in jail! Bear in mind that: 2,528 British nationals were detained overseas during 2005, a third of them for drugs-related offences; many countries outside the UK refuse to grant bail before trial and may detain people in solitary confinement; you will still get a criminal record in the UK if arrested with drugs abroad; if you've been caught with drugs abroad, you're unlikely ever to be allowed to visit that country again.

3. Passports, Visas and Work Permits

If you wish to travel abroad you must hold a full ten-year passport, even for a day trip. Apply in good time. In the UK, you can get advice from the Identity and Passport Service website at www.passport.gov.uk or call them on 0870 521 0410 (lines are open 24 hours a day and calls are charged at the national rate). Some countries have an immigration requirement for a passport to remain valid for a minimum period (usually at least six months) beyond the date of entry to the country. Therefore, if appropriate, ensure your passport is in good condition and valid for at least six months at the date of your return. This is a requirement of the country concerned, not the UK Passport Service, and any questions should be addressed to their Consulate or Embassy.

Outside the UK, you should get advice in an emergency from the nearest British Embassy, High Commission or Consulate. Staff can issue standard replacement passports in most places, and all missions are able to issue emergency passports if more appropriate.

If you plan to travel outside British territories, you may require a visa to enter the country you are going to. Check visa requirements with your project organiser or travel agent or contact the Consulate or Embassy of the country you plan to visit.

If you plan to work outside the European Union, you will need to obtain a valid work permit before you go.

Some Passport Tips:

- Make a note of your passport number, date and place of issue (or take a photocopy), and keep separately in a safe place.
- Check your passport expiry date.
- Write the full details of your next of kin in your passport.
- Leave a photocopy with a friend or relative at home.
- Take a second means of photo-identification with you.
- Keep your passport in the hotel safe and carry a photocopy with you.
- If your passport is lost or stolen overseas, contact the nearest British Embassy, High Commission or Consulate immediately for advice.

4. Health

- Check the Department of Health website at: www.dh.gov.uk/en/Policyandguidance/Healthadvicefortravelle rs for general medical advice for travellers.

- Check what vaccinations you need with your GP at least six weeks before you travel.

- Check if your medication is legal in the country that you are visiting.

- Pack all medication in your hand luggage.

- If you are taking prescribed medication, take the prescription and a doctors letter with you.

- If you are travelling within the European Economic Area or Switzerland, you should get a free European Health Insurance Card (EHIC) by visiting the Department of Health website as above. You can also obtain the EHIC by completing the Department of Health leaflet 'Health Advice for Travellers' (HAFT), available through most UK Post Offices or by telephoning 08701 555 455. The EHIC entitles you to free or reduced-cost medical care but you will still need medical and travel insurance.

- Be safe in the sun. Avoid excessive sunbathing, especially between 11am and 3pm, and wear a high factor sunscreen.

- Drink plenty of water. If you drink alcohol or use some kinds of drugs your body can become dehydrated, especially in a hot climate.

- Find out the local emergency number and the address of the nearest hospital when you arrive overseas. Your rep, local guide or project manager should know.

5. Safety

Be aware of what is going on around you and keep away from situations that make you feel uncomfortable. Avoid potentially dangerous 'no-go' areas, in particular after dark. Use your common sense and make sure you are constantly assessing and reassessing your personal safety. Be aware of drugs - these have been used in incidents of rape, so keep your wits about you.

Keep an eye on your possessions. Never leave your luggage unattended or with someone you don't completely trust. Be aware of pickpockets, who tend to operate in crowded areas, and lock up your luggage with padlocks. Make sure you have copies of all important documents such as your passport, tickets, insurance policy, itinerary and contact details. Keep these separate from the originals and leave copies with your family and friends.

Work out how much money you'll need on a daily basis and work to a realistic budget. Be sure to take enough money, as the Foreign and Commonwealth Office can't send you home free if charge if you run out!

Finally, tell friends and family your plans before you go and keep in regular contact, especially if you change your plans. Consider taking a roam-enabled mobile and use text or email to keep in contact. Don't promise too much - promising to call home every day is unrealistic and will only cause your family and friends to worry when you don't!

Further Information

For further advice on all travel, health and safety issues and more, visit the Go Gap Year website at: **www.gogapyear.com**

InterHealth specialises in providing detailed and specific travel health advice tailored to remote and exotic destinations. Its website includes a section for gap year travellers, with a particularly useful downloadable list of Dr Ted's Top Ten Tips before going abroad. The online shop can supply everything from first aid kits to mosquito nets and water purification tablets. **www.interhealth.org.uk/gap.htm**

Your school or college may be willing to organise a safety and security awareness training course to help you prepare for a gap year. One organisation specialising in this type of work is Objective Team. Visit their website at: **www.objectivegapyear.com**

For general advice on volunteering, visit the website at: **www.need2know.co.uk/work/volunteering**

If you are looking for a way of quantifying your gap year experiences to get the credit you deserve for your learning in a form that universities or potential employers would value, you might consider enrolling with an organisation called Gap Profile. For a fee of £250, you will be able to follow the Gap Profile programme, consisting of 10 open learning guides that take you through the process of self-analysis, objective setting and planning your own development. It should help you reflect on your experiences and collect evidence to demonstrate your development. Successful completion will enable you to earn the award of a City & Guilds Profile of Achievement. For full details, visit the website at: **www.gapprofile.co.uk**

Specialists in cheap flights, adventure trips and travel deals for young people, STA Travel have several pages of gap year travel tips on their website at: **www.statravel.co.uk**

Youth hostels can provide you with reliable, reasonably priced accommodation in many parts of the world. Hostelling International is the brand name of more than 90 Youth Hostel Associations in over 80 countries, operating 4,000 plus hostels. Unlike bland motels, impersonal hotels or dodgy backpacker rooms, youth hostels are usually fun, lively meeting places, full of like-minded people. Visit the website at: **www.hihostels.com**

Suggested Reading List

Suggested Reading List

Before You Go: The Ultimate Guide to Planning your Gap Year
- Tom Griffiths, Bloomsbury, 2003

The Gap Year Book: The Definitive Guide to Planning and Taking a Year Out (Lonely Planet Gap Year Guide)
- Joseph Bindloss and Charlotte Hindle, Lonely Planet Publications, 2005

The gap year guidebook 2007
- Alison Withers, John Catt Educational, 2006

Taking a Gap Year: The Essential Guide to Taking a Year Out
- Susan Griffith, Vacation Work Publications, 2005

Don't Tell Mum: Hair-raising Messages Home from Gap-year Travellers
- Simon Hoggart and Emily Monk, Atlantic Books, 2006

The Gap Year Handbook: An Essential Guide to Adventure Travel
- Tim Beacon, Authorsonline, 2005

Gap Year Volunteer: A Guide to Making It a Year to Remember
- Summersdale Publishers, 2006

Backpacker's Bible: Your Essential Guide to Round-the-World Travel
- Suzanne King and Elaine Robertson, Robson Books, 2005

Travel Health In Your Pocket
- Dr Ted Lankester, InterHealth

Worldwide Volunteering
- Worldwide Volunteer Organisation, How To Books, 2004

Green Volunteers: The World Guide to Voluntary Work in Conservation
- Fabio Ausenda, Vacation Work Publications, 2005

World Volunteers: The World Guide to Humanitarian and Development Volunteering
- Fabio Ausenda and Erin McCloskey, Vacation Work Publications, 2003

Archaeo-Volunteers: The World Guide to Archaeological and Heritage Volunteering
- Fabio Ausenda and Erin McCloskey, Vacation Work Publications, 2003

Improve Your Grades!

The following independent colleges offer specific retake and intensive revision courses, giving you the opportunity to improve your performance in a wide range of subjects during the Easter vacation.

Abbey Colleges

The Abbey Colleges are part of the Alpha Plus Group - formerly Davies, Laing and Dick Education Group - which currently comprises twenty independent schools, colleges and sixth form colleges, Lyn Fry Associates and the Best Practice Network. Abbey Colleges in Birmingham, Cambridge, London and Manchester offer intensive retake courses for GCSE and AS and A-Level.

www.abbeycolleges.co.uk

Ashbourne Independent Sixth Form College, Kensington, London

Easter revision courses seek to motivate students to strive for the highest grades at A level and GCSE, and to develop independence and self-reliance. As a private college, Ashbourne is able to offer classes which average five students per group.

www.ashbournecoll.co.uk

Bosworth Independent College, Northampton

Relatively new in terms of tradition, Bosworth Independent College boasts an ever growing reputation for academic excellence, providing Easter revision in addition to GCSE, A level, University Foundation Programmes and English Language courses

www.bosworthcollege.com

Cambridge Centre for Sixth-Form Studies

Easter Revision courses can make a major difference to your examination prospects. Classes are very small and teachers are experienced not just in covering the common core in each subject, but also the requirements for each specification.

www.ccss.co.uk

Collingham College, Kensington, London

Intensive tuition in small classes enables individual needs to be met. Groups are Board-specific as appropriate and are formed according to syllabus, topics, texts and so on. The courses are planned to give a clear understanding of the essentials of the syllabus and to teach exam techniques, so that you can use your knowledge to best effect.

www.collingham.co.uk

Davies Laing and Dick College, Marylebone, London

Easter Revision courses were introduced at Davies Laing and Dick College over 20 years ago to provide intensive tuition for extra mural students preparing for GCSE and A Level exams. The aim of Easter Revision is not only for you to become secure in your subject knowledge but also for you to become confident at taking exams efficiently. Exam technique, a skill sometimes neglected in schools, is given much emphasis.

www.dldcollege.co.uk/cms

d'Overbroeck's College, Oxford

For over 20 years the d'Overbroeck's Sixth Form has extended its approach to include GCSE and A level revision courses. It teaches in small classes, offers a wide range of subjects and is renowned for its teaching.

www.doverbroecks.com

Duff Miller Sixth Form College, South Kensington, London

Duff Miller offers Easter Revision courses across a wide range of A Level and GCSE subjects. They act to inspire, motivate and fulfil academic potential. The primary emphasis of the revision courses is to enhance subject knowledge and establish a rigorous, disciplined and effective approach, resulting in peak exam performance.

www.duffmiller.com

Harrogate Tutorial College

Easter Revision courses at Harrogate are designed to help students achieve examination grades well above those they originally expected, but are not intended for students who have done little or no work in their subjects. The small classes, average four, maximum eight students, generate an informal, student centred approach with the emphasis on high quality work.

www.htcuk.org

Justin Craig Education

Justin Craig Education offer revision courses in all the main AS /A2 and GCSE subjects at a choice of 10 residential or day centres around the country. Teachers ensure that all students are given the necessary assistance and motivation to revise quickly and productively.

www.justincraig.ac.uk

Lansdowne College, London

Lansdowne College has run Easter Revision courses for over 20 years, helping thousands of students to realise their full academic potential at both GCSE and A Level, and enabling them to progress onto their chosen path for their studies. Students often find themselves unaware of exactly what the examiners are looking for and subsequently unsure of what makes an A grade answer. The Easter Revision courses remedy this by not just focusing on the subject content, but also on extensive and comprehensive examination preparation, including a free mock examination at the end of the course.

www.lansdownecollege.com

Mander Portman Woodward (MPW)

MPW is an independent sixth-form college group, with colleges in London, Birmingham and Cambridge. In addition to full-time GCSE courses, AS courses and A2 courses over a very wide range of subjects and with no restrictions on subject combinations, MPW offers intensive A level and GCSE retake courses and revision courses over Easter. Characterising all courses is an absolute maximum of eight students within any one class and a strong emphasis on exam technique and exam practice.

www.mpw.co.uk

Millfield School, Somerset

On its Eater Revision course, Millfield offers specialist tuition at GCSE, AS and A2 level, in a broad range of subjects to small groups of students, providing a balance of taught content and rehearsal of technique. Students from all schools are welcome. Courses are offered on both a residential and non-residential basis.

www.millfieldenterprises.com

Oxford Tutorial College

Oxford Tutorial College organises short intensive revision courses at Easter and supplementary teaching to support the work being done at school. There is a mixture of individual tuition and small group seminars.

www.otc.ac.uk

Rochester Independent College, Kent

Intensive Easter revision courses at Rochester provide an opportunity to gain an overview of the syllabus and a chance to practise applying knowledge to real examination questions. This helps with recall of facts and hones skills required for accurate question interpretation and structuring full and concise answers. Most importantly, the courses give a real confidence boost at a crucial time.

www.rochester-college.org

Taster Courses, Summer Schools and Open Days

Almost all universities and colleges organise pre-application Open Days, giving you an opportunity to visit the campus, meet some of the staff and students, and attend a short talk on a subject in which you are interested. Details of these days can be found in the *Open Days* booklet, compiled by COA and published by UCAS.

We focus here on courses that some universities and colleges provide to give you a more detailed opportunity to experience academic and social life on campus. Please note that we refer to *Taster Courses* for the sake of clarity but universities are independent institutions and don't always use the same terminology. It is, therefore, not unusual to find *Taster Courses* described as Summer Schools or Academies (at any time of year!), Campus Days or Find Out More Days.

Duration

Course lengths vary: some are one-day courses only, others may last a weekend or even a week. Most courses are free. You may have the chance to stay overnight on campus.

Format

Most *Taster Courses* include lectures, discussions and tutorial sessions, so that you can meet the departmental staff and get hands-on experience using the facilities. This can provide an important insight into how the university or college operates. *Taster Courses* should also allow you to find out about other aspects of undergraduate life, such as sporting, musical, drama and cultural activities, accommodation and other amenities.

Benefits of Attending a Taster Course

- You are more likely to choose a higher education course to suit your interests and abilities and to avoid an unsuitable one.
- You can highlight your attendance in the personal statement section of your UCAS application.
- You may find that a course or campus is not for you, and decide to reject it in favour of others.
- You can discuss your impressions with admissions tutors at universities or colleges during interviews.

Science and Technology tasters

In addition to the Taster Courses listed on the following pages, see pages 36 and 37 for details of the science and technology tasters organised by Headstart and the Smallpeice Trust.

University of Aberdeen Summer School for Access

The Summer School is a ten-week, full-time programme, which runs from June to August each year. You have to undertake four courses and complete coursework and exams, on successful completion of which you will be guaranteed a place on an undergraduate programme at the University of Aberdeen. You may also use the Summer School for entry into other universities across the UK, although you must contact the other institutions and agree their entry requirements before you start.

If you are a student from within the European Union, you are not required to pay tuition fees for the Summer School and free accommodation may also be available.

For full details, email: SSA-Aberdeen@abdn.ac.uk

University of Wales Aberystwyth

The Marketing and Recruitment Office can organise workshops and open days relating to specific subject areas. For details, email: marketing@aber.ac.uk

Aston University

Aston organises a programme of events aimed at providing a taster of university life in specific subject areas, including: Biology, Business (Marketing), Business (Psychology), Computing, Chemistry, English Language, Modern Foreign Languages (French, German, Spanish), Psychology, Public Policy, and Sociology.

Contact Schools and Colleges Liaison for further information and dates at: aimhigher@aston.ac.uk

University of Birmingham School of Engineering

Free one-day taster courses in Engineering can prove ideal in helping you decide on which specialism and maybe which university. Birmingham offers the following programme each July: Chemical Engineering (last year's course included seeing how roasting of barley is modelled to ensure a perfect pint of beer every time!), Civil Engineering, Electronic, Electrical and Computer Engineering, Mechanical Engineering, and Metallurgy and Materials

For full details, visit the website at: www.eng.bham.ac.uk/sixth.htm

Bradford University Academy Compact Scheme

The Compact Scheme, part of the Bradford University Academy, provides sixth form students with a programme of activities, including support for your current studies, the opportunity to sample future degree options and help with your university application. The scheme can also help with progression to the University of Bradford by giving you the opportunity to complete additional work to obtain 30 points towards your Bradford UCAS tariff points offer.

Further information can be found on the website at: www.brad.ac.uk/compact

University of Chichester

Several departments at the newly-created University of Chichester run taster days, in which you can sample lectures or participate in workshops. In some cases, these events are open to all prospective applicants, while others invite people who have already applied, to help them make their final choice. You can book online for taster days - usually held in March/April - in the following areas: Business and IT Management,

Cultural Studies (English, History, Media and Theology), Sport Science and Sports Studies, and Youth and Community Work

Further information can be found at:
www.chiuni.ac.uk/tasterdays/index.cfm

Crichton University Campus, Dumfries

An access to university course runs on the Crichton Campus each year, lasting for anything between two and seven weeks. The purpose of these courses is to provide you with the skills and confidence to consider degree level study as a full- or part-time student, providing a taste of some of the subjects taught at university, along with a selection of skills based classes. Attendance can vary from part-time evening to full-time day courses.

To receive further information about the access courses, email:
admissions@crichton.gla.ac.uk or **crichton@paisley.ac.uk**

University of Exeter

The University's Schools and Colleges Liaison Service can invite students to pre-taster courses for Engineering, Maths and Physics.

To find out more, visit the website at: **www.ex.ac.uk** or email:
visitus@exeter.ac.uk

University of Exeter, Cornwall Campus Open Days

At Exeter's Cornwall Campus, near Falmouth, you can spend a day attending sample lectures, talking to academics about the courses and chatting with students about their experiences of life in Cornwall. There are also tours of the campus and student facilities, including the halls of residence, student bar and sports centre. Prospective Geology and Mining Engineering students can go down a real mine - the only one that is part of a UK university. New degrees in Law, Politics and History and the world's first undergraduate degree in Cornish Studies are on offer, adding to the range of subjects already available, which includes Biology, Geography, English and Renewable Energy.

For full details, visit the website at:
www.uec.ac.uk/studying/visiting.htm

Harper Adams University College

If you are considering a degree or HND in one of the agricultural–, animal–, food– or rural-based subjects, you may wish to attend the Harper Adams annual Higher Education Choices (HEC) conference in July. The two-day residential conference for students aged between 16 and 18 years has been running for over 20 years, with a range of industry representatives and university advisers able to advise on all courses and related career opportunities, from plough to plate. Overnight accommodation is provided in Harper Adams' own halls of residence, giving you a real taste of university life. The conference fee, including all meals, accommodation, entertainment, group photograph and the HEC polo shirt, is just £25. Apply with a friend and you pay £35 in total.

For further information and an application pack, email:
sbishop@harper-adams.ac.uk or log on to:
www.harper–adams.ac.uk/hec

University of Leeds

In addition to the University Open Days, you can also visit departments throughout the year, where you'll be able to take a more detailed look at resources and facilities. Details are available on their departmental web sites.

To find out more, visit the website at:
www.leeds.ac.uk/students/opendays/index.htm

London Taster Course Programme

With over 150 courses in 70 different subject areas, the London Taster Course Programme provides the opportunity to experience life as a university student in the subject area of your choice, ranging from medicine and dentistry to drama and film studies. The taster courses run from half a day to one week, and are usually available between March and July. All courses are non-residential and provided free of charge. You may apply for up to four courses via the online application form. The University of London administers the programme, with colleges participating as follows:

Central School of Speech and Drama
    Choices In Drama
    Voice

Courtauld Institute of Art
    Art and its Histories

Goldsmiths
    Anthropology
    Politics Today

Imperial
    Diagnosis of an Unknown Disease
    Physics
    Chemistry
    Computing

King's
    French
    German
    Film
    Humanities
    Mathematics
    Computer Science
    Ancient Art and Archaeology
    Archives and Corporate Records
    Nursing
    Midwifery

Nutrition
Medicine

London School of Economics and Political Science (LSE)
Geography and Environment
Government and Politics
Social Policy
Sociology

Queen Mary
Law
Business and Management
Working as a Dentist
Working as a Doctor
Film
Shakespeare
History
Human and Physical Geography
Solving Environmental Problems
Living Languages
Materials In Medicine/Dentistry
Materials In Forensics
Sports Materials
Materials Selection in Design
Mobile Music Videos: Engineering the Downloads
Chemistry
The Molecules of Life
Strings, Particles and the Nano-World
Computers
Mathematics
Women in Engineering
Aerospace Engineering
Design and Innovation
Mechanical Engineering
Medical Engineering
Sports Engineering

Royal Holloway
Biosciences
Science and Communication
Geography
Languages
Politics and International Relations
Philosophy
Mathematics
Computer Science
Economics
History

Royal Veterinary College
Veterinary Medicine

St George's
The Scientific Basis of Medicine

School of Oriental and African Studies (SOAS)
>Languages and Culture
>Arts and Humanities
>Politics and International Studies
>Law

The School of Pharmacy
>The Science of Medicine

UCL
>Women In Mathematics
>Experiencing the Ancient World
>History and Empire
>Archaeology
>Engineering Quality of Life
>Electronic Engineering
>Chemical Engineering
>Construction
>Exploring the Planets

The programme also includes a further seven universities in the London area:

City
>Business and the City
>Radiography
>Nursing and Midwifery
>Optometry
>Psychology
>Sociology
>Speech and Language Therapy
>Print Journalism
>Radio Journalism
>Music
>Computing
>Engineering
>Automotive Engineering
>Aeronautical Engineering
>Computing, Electronics and IT Related Subjects

East London
>Anthropology

Greenwich
>Games and Multimedia
>Mobile Computing
>Mathematics

London Metropolitan
>English
>Spanish
>French
>Applied Translation
>Graphic Design
>Computer Animation

Civil Aviation
Sports Therapy
Economics
International Relations
Psychology
Sociology
Forensic Science
Law
Business Administration
Business Law
Mobile & Wireless Computing
Business Information Technology

London South Bank
Product Design
Computing in the Information Age
Business and Management
Nursing and Radiography
Sports Exercise Science
Forensic Science

St Mary's College
Film and TV Studies

Westminster
Law

All courses are listed in the 36-page London Taster Course Programme brochure, which should be read online in conjunction with the regularly updated list of places available. You should note that the five-day medical courses at King's, St George's and The School of Pharmacy are exceptionally popular and fill rapidly.

Visit the website at: **www.london.ac.uk/tasters** or email: **tastercourses@london.ac.uk**

Myerscough College

At its main campus in Preston, the College offers a series of one-day HE taster events, designed to provide you with an opportunity to appreciate the courses available in such areas as: Agriculture, Animal Care (including Animal Behaviour and Welfare), Arboriculture, Ecology/Conservation, Equine Studies, Floral Design, Garden Design, Horticulture, Landscape, and Veterinary Nursing. These free events are open to anyone aged 16 or over, including mature students who are considering Higher Education.

For further information, email **schools@myerscough.ac.uk** or visit the website at: **www.myerscough.ac.uk**

Newcastle University

Each year, the University runs a series of taster events, workshop sessions, degree shows and public lectures, covering subjects such as architecture, engineering, sciences and fine art. You are given the opportunity to experience the University's teaching and facilities by attending demonstrations and/or short lectures in your chosen subject.

For details, email: **enquiries@ncl.ac.uk**

North East Wales Institute of Higher Education (NEWI)

Taster days at NEWI are designed to help you if you have not yet made the decision to enter higher education (HE). The focus is on demystifying HE, increasing awareness of the opportunities available, answering questions about finance and support, building confidence and skills, and getting to know the campus and facilities.

For further details, contact the Widening Access Team at **wideningaccess@newi.ac.uk** or visit the website at: **www.newi.ac.uk**

University of Reading Food Biosciences Summer School

Are you a young scientist with an interest in a career in food? The Department of Food Biosciences at Reading offers an annual short introductory course in early July for lower 6th form students (Year 12). The course is sponsored by manufacturing and retail companies in the food industry.

For further information, contact the Summer School Secretary at: **e.v.gillham@reading.ac.uk**

Royal Agricultural College (RAC)

The RAC's two-day taster course is aimed mainly at 16 to 19 year-olds but it may also be of interest to more mature students. It gives an insight into the career opportunities that exist in the food and land-based industries, both in the UK and worldwide. It also provides an opportunity to learn more about the courses on offer at the College. The cost of the course is £35, including accommodation and meals.

For full details, email: jenny.maguire@rac.ac.uk or visit the website at: **www.rac.ac.uk**

University of Southampton

The University holds some subject specific Open Days, which can provide you with an opportunity to visit a particular Academic School before completing your UCAS form. You will be able to meet staff and see the facilities. Academic School Open Days are currently offered by: Winchester School of Art, the School of Geography, and the School of Nursing and Midwifery.

Full details can be found on the website at: **www.soton.ac.uk**

Sparsholt College

If you are considering a career in the land-based or animal industries, Sparsholt offers broad-based taster course programmes for year 11 and sixth former students (two-day residential at Easter) and, for more mature students, taster-Saturdays in March and June. These special programmes all carry a nominal cost, but can be valuable in helping to make course and career choices.

Full details can be obtained by emailing:
enquiry@sparsholt.ac.uk

University of Surrey

The University organises a residential Summer School each year, with free courses designed to enable sixth-form students to taste what it's like to be a student in Higher Education. The Summer School includes tasters in a range of science and engineering subjects, in which students can experience both lecture type sessions and hands-on practical sessions. Past summer schools have seen students work in the Physics, Maths, Computing, Biomedical Science, Chemistry, Mechanical and Aerospace Engineering, Civil Engineering, Chemical Engineering and Electronic Engineering departments. They have been involved in activities such as: lectures on 'Black holes, Wormholes and Time Travel', running a chemical production plant, and finding out about Forensic Science.

For more information, contact the Educational Liaison Centre on 01483 689392 or email: **wp@surrey.ac.uk**

Swansea University

In addition to the Open Days organised by Swansea University, the Department of Childhood Studies holds its own individual day-long events to offer prospective students the opportunity to find out more about what being a Childhood Studies student is all about.

For full details, telephone 01792 518674 or email: **Childhood.Studies@swansea.ac.uk**

Taster courses may be available in other subject areas. For details, email the Student Recruitment Office at: **sro@swansea.ac.uk**

University of Teesside Summer Courses

You can get a taste of university life or develop essential skills for study or employment with a summer course at the University of Teesside. These free courses normally run during June, July and August.

Courses are available in areas including: Art and Design, Business, Education, English, Health, History, Information Technology, Languages, Law and Crime, Mathematics, Media, Psychology and Sociology, Science, Sport, and Youth Studies.

Students at Summer University have full access to books, including borrowing rights, and computers in the Learning Resource Centre. Other support facilities available during the summer include academic support in the Drop-In Student Skills Centre and personal counselling in the Student Centre.

For more information about Summer University short courses, call 01642 342291 or email: **summer.university@tees.ac.uk**.

The University also runs a series of 'Find Out More Days', in subject areas including Forensics, Health, Business, Psychology and Sociology, Art and Design, English and History, Sport, Computing, and Youth Studies.

Details can be found on the website at: **www.tees.ac.uk**

Wales Summer University

The Summer University provides a free six-week, full-time, residential (or non-residential) programme for young people in Wales. The programme consists of

Core Skills together with academic modules including Ancient History, Anthropology, Archaeology, Art, Business Studies, Biological Sciences, Computing and IT, Countryside Recreation, Creative Writing (in English), English Literature, European Languages, Film and Media Studies, The World and New Religions, Environmental Studies and Geography, History, Horse Management, International Politics, Law, Management, Mathematics, Organic Agriculture, Philosophy & Ethics, Physics, Psychology, Welsh

All students who successfully complete the Wales Summer University will be offered a guaranteed progression route to an appropriate degree scheme at the University of Wales Lampeter or Aberystwyth on condition that 2 A levels (or equivalent) are passed at grade E or above.

For full details, visit the website at:
www.lamp.ac.uk/summeruni/schools.htm

Note: this index relates primarily to activities mentioned in our brief descriptions of opportunity providers on pages 4 to 48. We cannot guarantee to have covered in just a few words every activity offered by every provider and we, therefore, recommend that you research thoroughly each project or organisation in which you are interested.

*   *Please note that some institutions do not list specific subjects for taster courses. We therefore suggest that you study pages 69 to 81 to see if a campus you would like to visit is included.*

Organisation	Page Number	UK	International	Paid	Volunteer	Adventure	Conservation	Community Work	Environment	English Teaching	Expeditions	Health	Home Stay	Language	Projects	Sport	Teaching	Variety of Opportunities	Working Holiday
Kibbutz Representatives	13		X	X								X						X	X
Lean on Me	14		X		X													X	
Learn Overseas	14		X								X				X	X		X	
Madventurer and Sportventurer	23		X		X			X		X								X	
Millennium Volunteers	14	X			X			X											
National Trust	15	X			X		X		X										
Outreach International	15		X		X			X											
Outward Bound Trust	23	X	X	X	X	X					X								X
Oyster Worldwide	15		X		X		X	X									X		
Personal Overseas Development	16		X		X			X	X		X								
PGL Travel	16	X	X	X	X	X		X								X			
Prince's Trust Volunteers	16	X	X		X			X									X	X	
Project Trust	17		X		X					X									
Quest Overseas	23		X		X	X	X	X	X	X	X			X	X				
Raleigh International	24		X		X	X	X	X									X		
REACH	17	X			X														
Students Partnership Worldwide	17		X		X	X		X											
Tall Ships Youth Trust	24	X	X													X	X	X	
Teaching and Projects Abroad	18		X		X			X	X							X	X	X	
The Leap Overseas	24		X			X		X	X							X		X	
Travellers Worldwide	18		X		X		X	X	X								X	X	
Trekforce Expeditions	25		X			X	X	X		X	X						X		
Ventureco	25		X			X					X			X					
Visit Oz	18		X																X
Voluntary Service Overseas	19		X	X				X										X	
Volunteering England	19	X	X		X			X										X	
Winant Clayton Volunteer Association	19	X	X		X			X											
Woodlarks Campsite Trust, Surrey	25	X																	
Worldwide Volunteering	20	Acts as a search and match service for UK and International projects																	
Year Out Group	20	Not for Profit association of UK registered organisations of well structured year out programmes